GW00683432

Introduction

Couching is quite simply a fabulous stitch, easy to sew and extremely versatile. It can be used to produce both delicate and bold effects offering an amazing range of surfaces. The word couching comes from the French verb 'coucher' which means 'to lie or set down'. In embroidery terms, to couch is to position threads on a fabric to create a pattern or image and sew them in place.

It is an ancient stitching technique that can be traced back at least as far as the 1st century B.C. where it was used on Scythian embroideries. A recurrent theme of the Double Trouble books is an emphasis on the importance of focus. In this book we are exploiting the technique of couching in its' many forms.

Couching is often listed as a line stitch where complicated, flowing or geometric designs can be stitched simply. It is sometimes referred to as the drawing stitch due to its linear qualities enabling designs to be outlined, highlighted or emphasised. When lines of threads are sewn adjacent to one another to make a solid or filled in area, this technique is called laidwork. It provides another versatile range of surfaces to consider.
Traditionally two needles and two threads are used to work most forms of couching. Generally, a heavier thread is laid on the surface and is stitched in place by a finer one.

The holding down stitch can be sewn at right angles to the main line, slightly angled or partially hidden depending on the effect envisaged. The more intricate the pattern, the closer the holding down stitches should be.

As shown on the following pages, the choice of the holding down yarn, its spacing and placing can be regular or irregular and can produce an array of complex or decorative surfaces.

Over the years, couched threads have been held in place by other well-known stitches such as cross, chain or herringbone stitches. These can look attractive if a formal pattern is required but would look too obvious or overwhelming if an organic textural surface were planned.

In this instance the holding down stitch may need to be toning in colour and as inconspicuous as possible. Normally, at the outset, the end of the laid down thread is taken through to the back of the fabric to be fastened securely with the finer thread and again when the stitching is completed. Using a stiletto or a large needle (Chenille 14), most yarns will pass through the cloth easily.

Couching facilitates the use of heavily slubbed, wired or highly textured yarns as these can be placed on top of the fabric without the struggle of attempting to pull them through from the back. This action could rip the cloth and more importantly damage or distort the thread. In most instances the thread ends could still be placed in a needle and eased to the back to secure them.
A firm fabric should be selected to support the weight of the stitches. A backing cloth could be used for a more delicate material.

Placing the material in a frame and keeping the cloth taut will help the stitching process and keep the lines true to the design unless wavy or loopy lines are required.

Illustrations on the following pages demonstrate an amazing range of threads and yarns now available. Wrapping, knotting, twisting or customising them suggest other exciting possibilities.

Exa wool, silk and metal threads decorating a wide range of artefacts can be viewed in many museum textile collections. Some date back to pre 10th century. Throughout history it has been a popular stitch and it continues to be so to the present day.

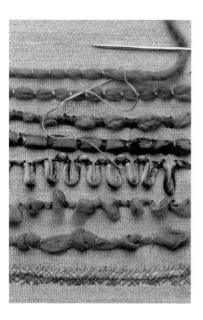

Above:

In this sample the first row shows the basic method using two needles.

For a clean linear effect it is best not to pull the stitching-down thread too tight.

In the second and third rows the thread has been pulled tighter to produce a bunched textured effect.

Variations of couching such as pendant couching will offer even more dramatic and raised dimensional possibilities.

Pendant couching involves placing the top thread in a series of loops and securing them with small couching stitches at the beginning and end of each loop. (See row 5).

The loops could lie flat or raised (row 6). When worked in groups they can form highly textured counterparts to the more linear aspects of the design.

Inside Front Cover: *The piece of work opposite celebrates all of the above techniques and uses a wide range of threads to achieve a textural monochromatic sample.*

Mixed Media Couching

Almost anything that can be placed on a surface of a fabric may be used for couching and in combination with the amazing array of conventional and commercial yarns there is a wonderful palette available. Torn fabrics are most effective when combining line with texture as well as being an excellent way of recycling materials.

The box top, brooches and small panels (above) demonstrate a colourful use of torn fabrics and recycled sari threads. When working small, closely worked couched shapes, it may be easier to start at the outside and work inwards as illustrated.

Household items such as paperclips, drinking straws, papers, wire, gift ribbons and feathers etc. could be stitched down with sympathetic or contrasting threads (top right). Bright synthetic colours can have dramatic impact on dark grounds.

Mixed media stitching is nothing new. Throughout history people have been endlessly inventive in using materials in their environment and couching has been a useful technique. North American tribes have used porcupine quills, feathers and bark in their textiles for centuries.

Left: A range of some of the threads that may be used for couching.

Plant materials are an excellent source for this couching. Dried leaves, grasses and twigs may be used to good effect. (bottom right)

Samples are of course a very good way of exploring new materials but when stitching more significant pieces it is advisable to consider the longevity and viability of the materials. There is no such constraint however when developing ideas through sampling and it is good to push out the boundaries as far as possible.

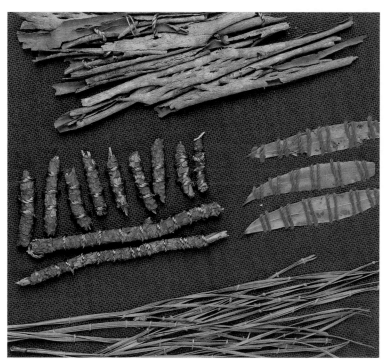

Designs from Natural Forms

It is always helpful to focus on particular aspects that surround us in every day life as observational skills definitely improve when there are certain elements to search for and track down. Surfaces that contain linear characteristics suitable for the technique of couching are abundant once our looking is tuned in.

Natural forms, their structures and growth patterns offer limitless possibilities. Cross-sections, stalks, twigs, veining, striations of every type could suggest a number of starting points. Wonderful ideas could develop from researching animal markings, patterns on caterpillars, butterflies, fish or bird feathers.

As shown, the stacked wood blocks found in builders' yard were particularly interesting. At first glance, the cross sections displayed beige and green colourings but on closer inspection more colours could be seen. Greatly enlarging the photograph on a photocopier revealed even more unexpected colours along with complex wood grain patterns. All the art-work shown has exagerated these aspects.

Top: Photo of wood blocks with a sample showing threads couched down by machine 'zig zag' stitches.

Above: Diagrams of simplified linear patterns.

Below: Design inspired by the blocks where the colour has been exaggerated using aquarelle crayons and pencils.

Right: Coloured paper shapes inspired by the above.

Couched samples:
1) rolled strips of silk fabric held in place with a variety of fine threads.

2) bold wool threads stitched with strips of torn silk.

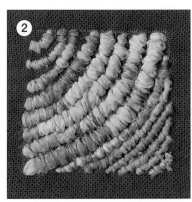

Many trees have wondrous bark patterns some of which sport long, deep, lichen encrusted fissures, crevices and ridges. A visit to a park, wood or an arboretum could be very inspirational. Initially, the tree illustrated did not appear to have obvious linear qualities. Eventually, lines of round dimensional shapes seemed to present an interesting challenge. Fabric strips were chosen to develop most of the samples shown and included rolled or frayed strips of silk and loosely knotted bandage gauze.

This Page: Aquarelle crayon and pencil drawing of a section of tree bark seen at Callaway Gardens, Georgia which inspired the adjacent sample.

Initially, loosely knotted bandage gauze was couched in place before bonded snippets, black polyester 'chiffon' and handstitching developed the surface further.

Water - A Mini Theme

Photograph by Jean Littlejohn

Sampling and exploring innovative materials and methods in abstract patterns is very satisfying but the challenge of a theme offers a different set of possibilities. When exploring new techniques and materials it is good to be open to the fresh opportunities they offer. In this way useful experience is gained. When working to a specific source of inspiration it is necessary to apply that experience in a more focused and disciplined way and with a fresh view on the subject.

We are surrounded by water in the form of rivers, lakes, oceans, seas and even swimming pools and ponds.

The colours and moods of water are hugely varied but the sinuous and sensual ripples and rhythms lend themselves beautifully to couching.

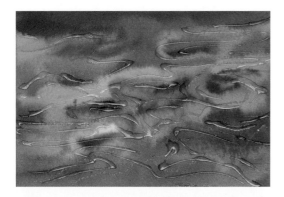

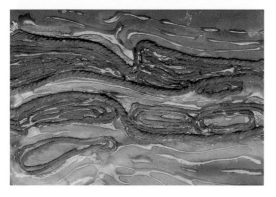

The surface of a swimming pool changes minute by minute and the patterns and colours reflect the surroundings. The ensuing patterns could provide a lifetime of study. Capturing the ephemeral patterns may be tried with sketching and photography but many attempts to record the patterns may be needed to capture the essence of the water.

Even though the patterns appear random there is a logic shown through the network and rhythm that begins to emerge with study. Look at the pool paintings and drawings of David Hockney and marvel at the apparent simplicity that he captures after years of careful observation of water.

A good way to start would be by collecting images and looking through holiday photographs where water often features.

Closer to home, the local swimming pool has wonderful surface patterns and colours.

When recording water images in sketchbooks, it may be helpful to use dye based products such as 'Koh-I-Noor' which will flood the page with pools of fluid colour. Wax crayons and oil pastels will offer the linear resists that describe the wave rhythms.

String and paper collage could also be used to good effect when designing for linear sources.

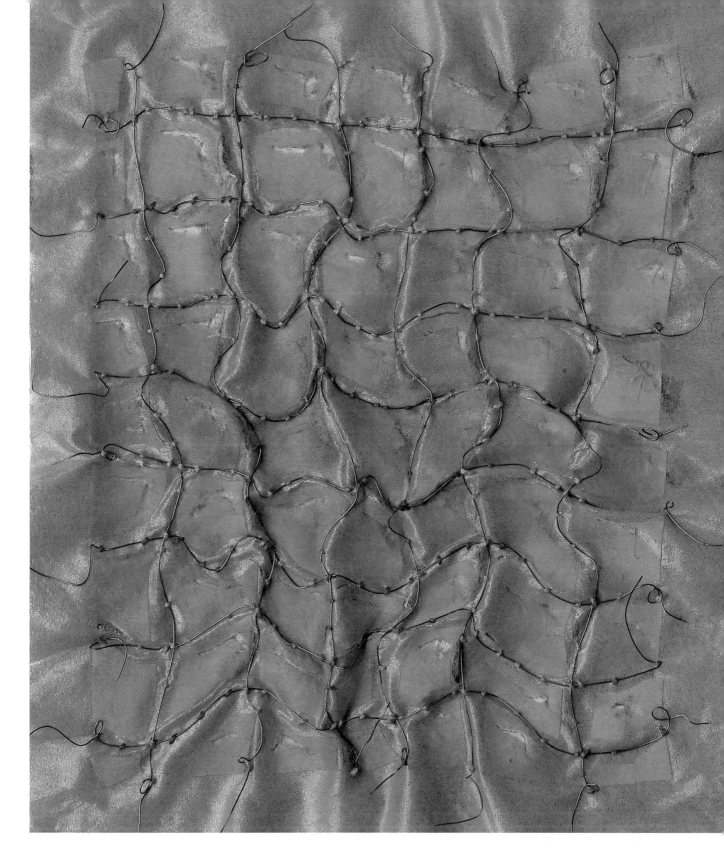

Top Left: Reflections on the surface of a swimming pool in evening light.

Far Left: 'Koh-I-Noor' dyes flooded onto water colour paper form the base for these patterns. Some colour was discharged using bleach. (When using bleach always wear gloves and a mask and work in a well ventilated space). The transparent linear lines were made by trailing PVA glue through a nozzle into water like patterns. Other lines were made with string and yarns.

The samples illustrated here demonstrate the versatility of couching.

Centre Left: It can be used to create solid areas of linear as seen

Above: The couched copper wire in this sample has formed a network based on swimming pool studies and it can be manipulated to produce dimensional surface effects.

The Mediterranean can be vibrant turquoise or inky blue depending on the time of day and circumstances. The surface may be calm, rough, or raked with gentle ripples.

The fractured water rhythms seen below are based on patterns on a painted boat seen reflected in the early morning calm sea in Tunisia. It has been a favourite image for some time but difficult to know how to interpret it.

Brief location sketches were attempted and being in water posed problems. In this case wax crayon and pencil were used, whilst standing in the water, to record the rhythms and the colour flooded in afterwards. (see left)

Photographs were another important element and wading into water with a camera can be a risky endeavour. It helps to wrap the camera securely in a watertight plastic bag and remove it carefully for the photographs.

Seeing the reflections in different conditions and times of day gave focus to the looking.

Pictured right is a range of samples exploring the various water patterns based on this source. They feature a variety of mixed media materials from gold wrapping paper and plastic straws through to pipe cleaners, and were inspired by the traditional method of *or nué*, a magnificent traditional technique used extensively in the past. Gold thread is couched down with coloured silks to make a shaded effect on the gold. It demands precision and immaculate working methods.

In the Middle ages, when pure beaten gold or silver threads often featured in ecclesiastical or special embroideries, couching was used extensively. It was particularly appropriate as it avoided the difficulty of working complex stitches with a stiff unwieldy thread and none of the precious metal was wasted.

The samples seen here are less labour intensive but explore colour and metal effects related to the rhythms of water. Wrapping paper, synthetic gold gift ribbon and fine sticky-back copper sheeting have been used to represent the bronze and gold highlights in the water. Zig zag machining over gold threads can also be effective.

The more resolved sample (far right) uses metallic pipe cleaners, gold and patterned plastic wrapping paper to form the basis of the rippled couching. The holding down stitches echo the rhythms of the fracture patterns and are worked in a range of silk threads.

Photograph by Jean Littlejohn

①

Bokhara & Romanian Couching

Unlike conventional couching, both these stitches are made by using only one needle and thread. A long straight stitch is made over the fabric and is held in place by oversewing it with the same thread on the return journey. It is the position of the holding down stitch that differentiates these two stitches. Bokhara couching has short oblique stitches crossing over to hold the line in position (see diagrams below). By contrast the Roumanian version is worked with long stitches, which cross over the line and are placed closely alongside the laid thread (see diagrams on page 13). In both versions, the laid down thread can be allowed a little slack to accommodate some variations from a straight line so that the holding down stitches on the return journey can position the top thread to form gentle curving shapes.

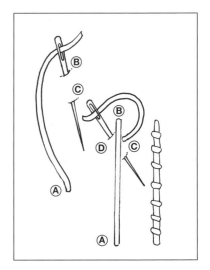

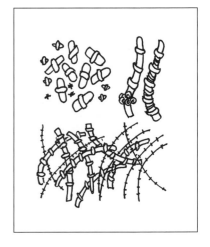

Bokhara and Romanian couching are ancient stitches that deserve great respect. Re-discovering or revising them can be most rewarding and will extend your stitch vocabulary.

Bokhara couching originates from Uzbekistan near north Afghanistan. The formalised patterns of flowers were very similar to those embroidered in Persia (Iran) and were mainly embroidered in silks to adorn magnificent costumes, bed covers and curtains. Due to the closeness of the stitches and the thickness of the threads used, the designs exploited embossed characteristics. This along with the sheen of the silk resulted in sumptuous embroidered cloths.

Romanian embroidery is known for its colourful designs made from repeating motifs and used to decorate clothing and household articles. In many well-respected stitch dictionaries there is some confusion over the spelling of the name. Roumanian is often used probably due to the popular enunciation. On looking though an old atlas, the index listed it with 'see Romania' next to it, thus the spelling that has been chosen for this book.

More complicated arrangements can be created by working shorter stitches to follow the shape of the motif or design and adding an extra holding down stitch to camouflage the joins.

In both cases, if the initial stitches are worked in bolder yarns or wool's these could support other lines worked on top to create organic type ridges or textures. Further lines can be stitched in a variety of threads adorned with beads or other mixed media materials as appropriate for the intended surface envisaged. Experimenting with unusual materials such as garden twines, cords or strips cut from plastic bags will further extend your choices.

Both couching stitches are fairly quick to work and if spacing, tension and layering of the stitch are considered, an amazing assortment of surfaces can be created. Although both share similar features, the resulting effects are very different.

With the wealth of fabulous threads now available, these stitches should be seriously considered.

Samples 1 & 2: show Bokhara couching worked in a variety of thick, thin. matt and shiny threads. The varying arrangements and layering demonstrate the versatility of this stitch.

3: The brooches and little box top motif show Bokhara stitch with beading worked over a machine-stitched mesh on soluble fabric. This method results in a non-fraying edge which negates the need to turn and finish edges necessary when dealing with a conventional cloth.

Above: *Dramatic geological markings incised into rock inspired the piece illustrated (above). The sample was worked mainly in Romanian couching and further developed using machine stitching with some wrapped areas for extra emphasis.*

Left: *sketchbook study of the rock using ink, paint and melted wax.*

The versatility of Romanian couching is illustrated by these samples worked in a wide range of threads and yarns. Endeavouring to experiment by varying threads, their placements and the layering will result in an amazing range of textural surfaces to consider for future works. NB. The shorter version of the couching, as shown, is listed as Romanian stitch in some stitch books.

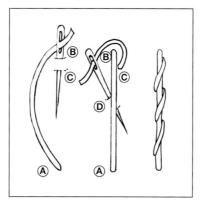
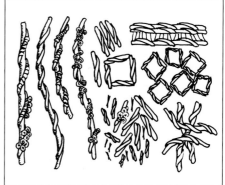

1: Lines worked in a variety of wool's and knitting yarns.

5: A simple set of line stitches where the initial straight stitch was allowed a little slack for a simple rhythmic effect.

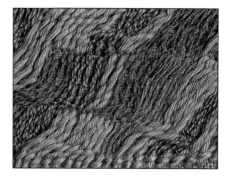

2: A range of threads, some of which support other lines of the stitch for dimensional effect.

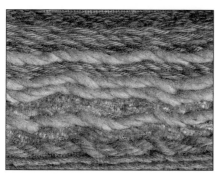

6: This sample shows the same starting procedure but worked in layers of heavier thread.

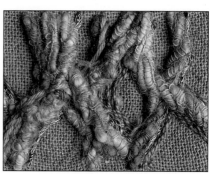

3: Short stitches were worked in thin and thick threads to form this arrangement. Some were layered and wrapped to develop the textural surface.

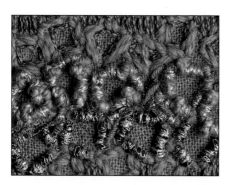

7: This simple arrangement exploits the quality of the yarns where the lustre or twist catches the light.

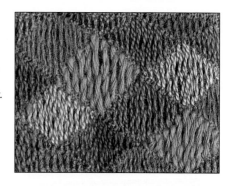

4: Thin and bolder yarns worked as very short stitches, many of which were wrapped to make interesting bundles reminiscent of bullion knots but easier and much quicker to do.

8: Short Romanian stitches worked with knitting yarns to form cross stitches which have resulted in a more robust surface.

Drawing for Couching

Although couching is a technique traditionally relying on linear design, we have seen from the previous pages that there are limitless other possibilities for this versatile stitching method.

Experimental and innovative samples might even encourage a more proactive approach to finding sources of inspiration. Seek out objects or groupings that might work well and perhaps the garden could be a good place to start as it is full of possibilities such as fencing, stalks and stems, trailing plants etc.

Garden centres also display a range of suitable collections. Piles of wood, trellis units and stacks of assorted items afford a wide range of opportunities.

Similarly, junk yards, with piles of old roof tiles and paving stones could be a marvelous source of inspiration. (see sketches right)

An old discarded bird nest proved a rich source of visual research with many interesting different combinations of line using mixed media. (see left)

A range of sketchbook studies pointed the way to innovative ideas and mixed media combinations. It is good to experiment with different media as each reworking of an image helps to move it into unexpected variations of line, colour, texture and composition.

1: A drawing based on fossilised plant forms inspired the couched sample seen right and on the cover.

2: Cotton cord has been couched down onto a partially felted wool and then placed into a washing machine on hot wash. During the wash the couched threads and background became distorted and imbedded and this formed an interesting base for further stitching and wrapping.

Landscapes

Landscape is always intriguing to observe as it provides inspiration from its many attractive, dramatic or atmospheric qualities. Linear patterns feature in abundance. Divisions between fields such as hedgerows, fences, ditches and irrigation channels all demonstrate a wonderful assortment of colour, pattern and texture. Tractor tracks, lines of crops or avenues of fruit trees may suggest other alternatives.

Close observation will reveal the many linear variations of growing or harvested crops. Initially, young plants such as grass, wheat or barley grow vertically in straight lines. As their growth progresses, different textural characteristics emerge and they may appear more wavy and curvy ruffled by a breeze.

When harvested, any short stubble that remains plus the debris stalks may suggest alternative patterning. The lines of ploughed fields with lumpy clods of soil or lines of winter grass peeping through a powdering of overnight snow are all areas to consider.

Understating or emphasising certain aspects will enable you to develop your own style and not be limited to copying a photograph and attempting to be too literal. Even if a little fearful, always try to sketch making accompanying notes as these will support your selection process which already starts at this stage. Everybody views things differently. Whatever appealed in the first instance is usually the aspect to concentrate on.

Some of the following notes were taken from a sketchbook and were helpful to re-kindle and highlight a memory. A photograph does not always capture your personal reaction.

'A steep hillside with overlapping lines of sun bleached stalks.'

'The torrential rain exaggerated the golden and burnt orange colour of rows of corn stalks.'

'Wavy, whispy, feathery grasses swaying in the wind.'

'Low sun shining on the bent ears of barley to give dramatic silver diagonal lines.'

'Stalks strewn and flattened by the tractor or harvester making complex criss cross patterns. They appear silver in the late evening sunshine.'

Right: Miniature interpretations of crops growing in two local fields at different times of the year.

Method

1: Conventional couching in the main where the holding down stitches have been placed closer to simulate the receding stalks. The bolder ones in the foreground show Romanian stitch worked in bolder twines and knitting yarns.

2, 3 & 4: A mix of conventional and Romanian couching in a range of paper string, wool, cotton, silk yarns. Metal threads have been used to highlight **3**

5 & 6: Short lengths of Romanian couching worked in weaving yarns and silk.

Left: Sketch painted with 'Koh-I-Noor' dye based colours, coloured crayons, pencils and texture gels textured the foreground.

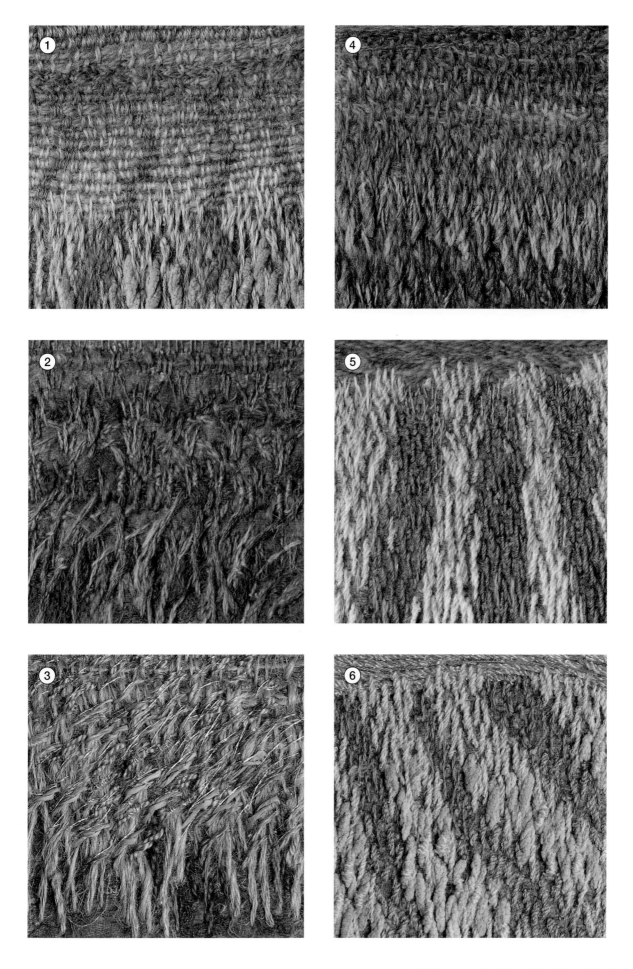

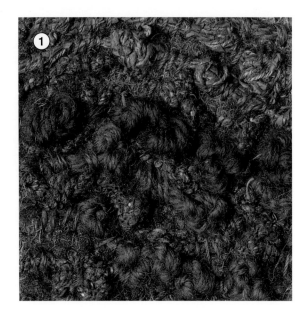

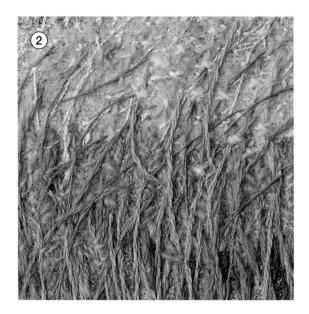

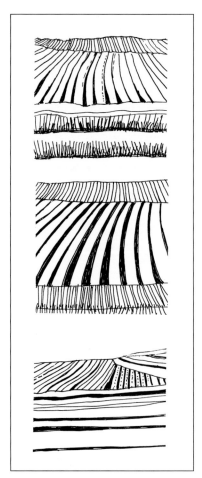

This page:

1: A ploughed field interpreted by couching threads that have been textured by knotting using the conventional method.

2: Romanian couching showing how delicate and bold effects can be achieved. These samples were developed from the sketches shown.

The simple line drawings show the suitability for this technique.

This panel 'Beyond the Brow' has been made by hand stitching on top of a grid which was machine stitched on soluble fabric in order to create a new cloth.

Romanian couched lines were used in the main as they result in stronger marks than straight stitches. Machine stitches were worked on top to embed the stitches to unify the whole piece.

Couching for Emphasis

Textures can be both rich and seductive but couching also makes dynamic marks.

The couched line can be used for strong dynamic committed marks or the most subtle willowy tracings. The placing of a strong mark within a composition can often pose more problems than piling up layers of texture.

Since the stitching may be dramatic and used for emphasis, place and pin the thread before committing. It is always a good idea to stand back and view the work from a distance or hold it up to a mirror to check on the work before proceeding.

Should it be necessary to embed threads into the background then this can be done by hand and or machine stitching to good effect. The work on these pages demonstrates the use of couching for emphasis within a composition.

Right: 'With love from'
This piece has been carried out in bonding techniques with printed and embellished surfaces. The couching is designed to give the work strength and a change of pace. In places, machine stitching has been used to bed it into it's background.

Left: *The wedding bag illustrates the use of couching to create definition on a highly textured surface.*

Very fine narrow old lace has been couched in a simple grid on to a silk ground. The hearts have been couched to add a strong raised focus before being encrusted with crystals and pearls to catch the light on the wedding day.

On the reverse of the bag, couching has been used to make the initials of the couple. The bag held a small booklet containing the 'something old' etc and in this case the 'something borrowed' was needles, threads and safety pins.